When you've lost your motivation and you're feeling kinda low,
pick up this book and find your place, the book will let you know.
And as you turn each page remember, you have come so far,
you know this stuff but let the words remind you who you are.

To…

From…

THE RIGHT WORDS

DONNA ASHWORTH

Author's Note

Welcome to my third book.
I have been overwhelmed with how much love you showed
to the women, I had no idea it would make such an impact.
I truly hope this one does the same and more.

It's quite simply full to bursting with little passages of hope,
comfort and joy.
From me to you.

As I always say,

*"the right words, in the right order, at the right time,
can do so very much."*

I hope you pick this up when you need a little something and let
the book decide which page you need to read today.
It's really good at that.

Thank you for buying this book,
or if you've been given it,
someone thinks you are pretty wonderful.
Isn't that a thing.

Donna

CONTENTS

PAPER PLANES

The words you type,
are little paper aeroplanes.
They travel further than you know.

Some land softly, delivering joy.
Some land with the sharpness of a dart...

Ripping out a little piece
of someone's heart.

The words you speak,
are little paper aeroplanes.
They do much more than you can see.

Some land lightly, with love.
Some land like a heavy fall from above...

The straw that breaks
the donkey's back.

Send your little aeroplanes out with care,
the world hurts enough.

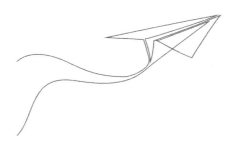

AS TIME GOES BY

As times goes by,
you will learn to see yourself more clearly,
the girl who was always too much of one thing,
and too little of another, was actually
everything she needed to be.
Let her out.

As time goes by,
you will let the simple things become the big,
and you will allow the big things to become the simple,
and that readjustment will be,
the day you really start to live,
Let it be.

As time goes by,
you will be forced to say goodbye many times,
and your soft little heart will shatter
but it will still beat and that will bring you,
all the purpose you need.
Let it beat.

As time goes by,
you will stop choosing wealth over peace,
you will stop choosing money over time,
and you will see that the treasures you need,
are in the smiles and the laughter.
Let them in.

As times goes by,
the moments you remember when your life flashes past,
are never the awful memories my friend, it's the joy,
the summer nights, the lazy days with loved ones,
the midnight chats and the morning hugs,
let them happen.
Let them all happen.

YOU'RE A WORK IN PROGRESS

You're a work in progress.
But you mustn't wait,
or apologise for who you are now.
You're exactly who you are meant to be, today.
Let those you love see *you*,
in all your unfinished glory.

And never apologise for not being done yet.

Remember,
every time you break, or fail, or mess up,
you are growing into the beautiful, unique person
you were always meant to be.

So reach and fail, fly and fall, love and lose.
It's as it should be and you are perfect,

Just the way you are.

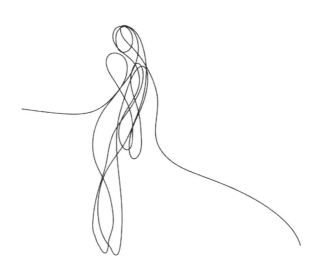

MAKE PEACE WITH YOUR BODY

Make peace with your body today my friend,
for it has toiled many years just to keep you alive.
It has grown, weathered virus and disease,
healed countless wounds and fought many unseen battles,
to keep your soul intact for its journey through this life.

Yes it has changed but striving against this change,
is like trying to blow away the wind,
futile, pointless, misery-making.
Your body has served you well and done so,
with your daily hate and disapproval.
It has suffered years of negativity,
pulsing its way from your brain to your cells.
Not good enough, not attractive enough, not perfect.

And every day you thought it wasn't perfect,
it really, truly was.
It was keeping you alive, supporting your rash decisions,
counteracting your foolish mistakes,
doing everything in its power to stay in the game.
For you.

Make peace with your body today, my friend,
say your apologies, right your wrongs
and move on with appreciation.
You are blessed.

Look around you, not everyone is so blessed.
Not every one is breathing, walking, thriving.
And whilst you are looking around, see that nobody is perfect.
The way a body looks, says nothing about its strength,
its longevity, its endurance.

This is not a rehearsal, this is your one shot at a beautiful life.
Make it count.

TO BE KIND

If you worry you're not kind enough,
then I think you're already so.
Because kindness is within you,
you just have to let it flow.

It's the wishing good on strangers,
even though your day is grey.
It's the smiling at the lady who,
is getting in your way.

It's the little spoon of sugar,
that you leave out for a bee.
It's the catching of a spider,
in a glass, to set it free.

It's the sending out good messages,
even though they're in your head.
That somehow works as well,
as if you'd texted it instead.

It's stopping for a stranger,
who is holding out a tin.
It's the not becoming blind,
to someone eating from a bin.

It's the writing of good wishes,
when a milestone has been met.
Not just birth and marriage,
maybe getting out of debt?

It's the sharing of your treasures,
whether plentiful or not.
To some, a pound means nothing,
but to many, it's a lot.

Continued...

It's the listening to the stories,
you have heard ten times before.
But refuse to show the signs,
that you're finding it a chore.

It's the trying to cut out plastic,
and eat more plants than meat.
Being kind to the planet,
and yourself, is no mean feat.

Kindness is a feeling,
an atmosphere of care.
It's not the great big gestures,
it's just showing that you're there.

If you're worried that you're not,
then my friend, you're off the hook.
For those who even think it,
are those who write the book.

ACCEPT NO SHADE

Not everyone will like you.
Not everyone will agree with the things you say, or do.
Not everyone will understand why you *are who you are,*
which trials and tribulations made you stronger,
weaker, braver.
Not everyone will care to look beneath, peek behind,
or read between.

That's ok.
Some people will.

Some people will find you so fascinating that they will delve
right into your depths.

Some people will devour your words and commit them to
memory, should they ever need to revisit them again,
in times of pain.

Some people will crave your company,
like a flower craves the rain.

Some people will not only appreciate your light
but they will reflect it right back.
They will charge you from the soul,
like being plugged into the sun.

They are *your people.*

Accept no shade from haters my friend,
life brings enough of that.

Always seek out the light.

LOVING YOURSELF

Loving yourself is a big ask.

To some, it may as well be a mountain covered in treacherous ice.
A journey too far,
a journey so overwhelming,
that finding the start point can often seem impossible.

Begin by showing yourself some slack every now and again,
move into a healthy mutual respect,
and then perhaps gravitate to treating yourself,
as you would a good friend.

Laugh at your own jokes,
see the life well-lived in each tummy roll
and be forgiving when you've made mistakes,
or behaved as every human does, *imperfectly*.

It's the least you would give to another,
so it shouldn't be too far a stretch.

Loving yourself is a big ask, so simply start with kindness,
the rest will come.

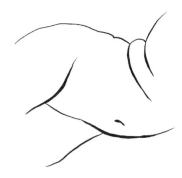

THE STITCH OR THE SCISSORS

Are you the stitch, or the scissors,
to that person's final thread?
The trouble is you'll never know until you snip.
So surely it's always better to stitch?

We are majestically chaotic creations,
of invisible, magical threads.
Some of us have stronger threads than others.
Some of us aren't gifted with enough thread from the start.
And some are thrown so quickly to the wolves,
that too many threads are cut at once.

So my friend,
be the stitch,
not the scissors,
to that person's precious threads.

Because we just don't know,
how many they have left.

I'VE BEEN YOUNGER, I DIDN'T LIKE IT

Maybe, we can be totally happy to 'look our age'
but still want to look great?

Maybe we can love to wear new make-up,
buy the latest clothes and try new looks
but we don't need anyone to tell us we look *younger*...

As though that's the goal.

It's not *my* goal my friend.

I have been younger my whole life,
it didn't make me happy then.

So perhaps I don't want to spend the best part of my life,
trying to look like something I have already *been*
and not liked very much at all.

I hated my body then,
yet it was 'perfect',
why would I want to chase that?

And what's more, I have spent many a year trying to look different;
better, blonder, thinner, curvier, smoother,
whatever society dictated that day.

I'm certainly not down for spending the most peaceful part of my
time here on this earth, chasing the youth,
I didn't even want when I had it.

Join me my friend,
let's look our age and let's do it in style.
We earned it.

TU ME MANQUES

The french don't say, 'I miss you',
they say **Tu me manques**,
'You are missing from me'.

You
Are
Missing.

I feel your absence as though I am lacking a vital part of my body
but for some reason, I continue to live on.
You are a vital part of my soul,
so I suppose that makes perfect sense.

They say that grief is simply the love you felt for that person,
roaring around in pain,
trapped inside your body,
with nowhere to go.

I have so much of that for you.
I have so much of it, I could open the windows
and let that roar encompass the world.

Tu me manques,

You
are missing
from me.

I'M IN THE RAIN

I'm in the rain,
I'm in the pain,
I'm in the blood within your veins.
I'm in the air,
My favourite chair,
I'm in the soulful way you care.
I'm in the night,
I'm in your sight,
I'm in your heart and holding tight.
I'm in the skies,
The children's eyes,
I'm in your sobs and in your sighs.
I'm in your life,
The cause of strife,
And that thought cuts me like a knife.
My darling one,
My moon, my sun,
Please don't let all I was become,
Your daily sadness,
Source of madness,
I used to be a font of gladness.
If you can hear,
When I am near,
Please let me take away the fear,
And bring back love,
I'm not above,
I'm close around you like a glove.
So breathe me in,
Let life begin,
Loss will fade but love must win.

YOU'RE NOT A PERFECT PARENT

You're not a perfect parent,
that much is true.
You shout sometimes,
you can be short-tempered and impatient.
You're not a perfect parent,
perfect parents don't exist.

But you are the only person in this world,
who can love your child exactly the way you do.
You see them, you know them, you *are* them.
Your connection is unique, your bond is unbreakable.
You would lay down in the road for them.
You eat, breathe and sleep them and no matter how distracted
you get or how short your fuse can be, they are loved.
And guess what, they know it.

Because your love is imprinted into every little cell in their bodies.
It came directly from your body and it goes so much deeper than
the troubles of the day.

And magically, we know not how, those parents who are not
biologically linked to their child, somehow become so.
The wonder of unconditional love does that.

It's intrinsic, built in, life-lasting.
It's real, raw, scientific, spiritual, genetic, unconditional, all-
consuming, *die-for-you* parental love.

So, forget how you failed as a parent today my friend.
No-one got it just right.

End the night with a cuddle filled with heart and soul
and all your foibles will be forgotten.

Because that's how love works.

CHILD YOU ARE A MAGNET

Am I funny?
Am I pretty?
Am I liked?
Your child will ask you one day.
And your mothering heart will rush to answer yes yes yes
but maybe that's the moment we should all begin to teach,
that none of it matters.

Perhaps we could say,

"My child, you are a mystical magnet all of your own design.
And you will attract into your life people who value you,
simply for being exactly who you are. It's science and nature
inextricably combined, in the most beautiful way

And sadly, some people will see something in you which upsets them,
perhaps because they want it, or perhaps they have been taught to fear
it. None of that is your fault nor your responsibility.

You must shine through life being exactly who you are,
regardless of how others label you,
it's the only way to wake up every day feeling at peace."

Maybe if we started this mantra very early,
we could save our beautiful, complex little humans,
so much sorrow and wasted energy...

Trying to fit in when they were born to stand out.

DON'T PRIORITISE YOUR LOOKS

Don't prioritise your looks my friend,
they won't last the journey.
Your sense of humour though,
will only get better with age.
Your intuition will grow and expand,
like a majestic cloak of wisdom.
Your ability to choose your battles,
will be fine-tuned to perfection.
Your capacity for stillness,
for living in the *now*, will blossom.
Your desire to live each and every moment,
will transcend all other wants.
Your instinct for knowing what (and who)
is worth your time, will grow and flourish
like ivy on a castle wall.

Don't prioritise your looks my friend,
they will change forevermore,
that pursuit is one of much sadness and disappointment.

Prioritise the uniqueness that make you *you,*
and the invisible magnet that draws in other like-minded souls,
to dance in your orbit.

These are the things which will only get better.

I WISH THEY WOULD TEACH THE GIRLS

I wish they would teach the girls in school...

That all bodies are different and some will never be happy at a low weight. It's a genetics thing, you'll have a life-long fight on your hands if you want to look like the girls on tv.

That the girls on tv are either genetically built that way or locked in a cycle of deprivation and misery to achieve a physical standard set by society.

That each body has its perfect size and weight and that self-love (cheesy but powerful) and good nutrition, is the way to get there. The *only* way.

That bodies are only one part of who you are and that to be honest, it's high-time we stopped letting our looks define us, we are so much more.

That even the girls who look like they have it all, have major self-doubts and insecurities. If we all shared this commonality, we would be unstoppable.

That perhaps the world does not want women to be unstoppable, hence the multi-million pound empires which feed from our body issues like vultures on a carcass.

I wish they would teach the girls in school that the worst thing you can be, is not fat or ugly...

The *worst* thing you can be, is locked forevermore, in a prison of your own self-doubt.

Things would be so different.

FREE SPEECH

The thing about 'free speech' is that it's not free.
You should not feel you can 'say whatever you want'.
Not if those words cost someone else.

Nothing is free.

Even love isn't free,
it costs that person to open up their heart
and if that love is not reciprocated,
the fall-out is catastrophic.

If that love is disrespected,
the cost is extremely high indeed.

Life-changingly so.

Free speech does not mean being allowed to open your mouth
and let the hate or ignorance rush out.

That stuff should be filtered first.

Examined for evidence of your own unsettled pain and trauma.
Researched for fact and truth.

Considered for the impact it may have on the vulnerable.

Then, only then, should you feel able to say it out loud,
put it in writing and send it out to the world.

Nothing is free.
There is always a cost.

LOVE ISN'T

Love isn't all hearts and flowers.
Sometimes, love is asking if you've remembered to take your
vitamins or drunk enough water.

Love is a friend who checks in on you,
even when you say you're *fine*.

Love is a family member,
who worries you're making the wrong choices.
That can often feel like anything but love but the truth is,
they live in fear of you getting hurt,
because they feel every inch of your pain along with you.

Love can come in all shapes and sizes but never does
unconditional love look like an expensive gift
or a romantic weekend away.
That's just frosting.

You're more likely to find it in a cup of tea,
made just for you.

Love is real and ugly and shouty sometimes.
Lots of tears and lots of pain as the people involved break and
bond and grow together as humans.

If you are loved my friend, at all, you are blessed.

And if you have found some love for yourself along the way,
you are really winning at life.

That's worth celebrating, on Valentine's Day or any other.

ONE TINY STEP

When things get tough, *really* tough, and you don't have the will,
the answers or the energy to fight anymore.
There is only one way to go,
forward...

One tiny, *tiny* step, at a time.
If you can't see the way forward, look,
quite simply, for the very next step and take that.

You're moving...
One tiny step at a time,
eat something,
read something,
watch something,
answer one text,
send one email,
shower.

Any of these steps will keep you moving and keep you afloat.
Congratulate yourself and rest.

Your body is not impervious to the stresses of the times
and your brain is often both overloaded and undernourished.

Your wellbeing thrives on freedom, sunshine, love, joy
and these are not always in plentiful supply.

So, one tiny step at a time my friend.

Do not add pressure to be perfect to your list of worries in this
life, there is no space for that.

THE VOICE

Listen to the voice that tells you no when something's off,
the prickle of your skin when something isn't what you thought.

Listen to the goosebumps, alongside something new,
the flutter in your gut when that path is right for you.

Listen to the friends who come inside when lights are low,
the ones who stay to clear when the party people go.

Listen if you must to the other friends you have,
but remember they are often not around when you are sad.

Listen to your elders if their smiles are wise and true,
they've many tales to tell and your worries they've been through.

Listen to the people life delivers at your feet,
the ones you've no idea, how you even came to meet.

Listen carefully to all the voices in your life,
but heed me when I say there is one who'll bring you strife.

That nasty little voice that seems to live inside your mind,
the one who says you're useless, the one who's never kind.

It's that voice you must beware of from your dawn until your dusk,
it wants you to feel worthless, wants to wear you down to husk.

A voice you made yourself when the world first broke your heart,
a voice that's yours to silence, so a brand new life may start.

WILD

Keep a little bit of you wild,
child.

That little part of you that seeks out the moon, the sunrise, the
waterfalls.

The part of you that craves the freshest of air, the thickest of
forests and the giant waves.

It's important.
For she is directly connected to the core of the earth,
the tides and the stars.
She is intrinsically linked to all creation,
to life itself, to existence.

Don't let the modern world push her out,
she is wild and she is free and you need her,
to be the you, you were always meant to be.

Keep a little bit of you *wild,*
child.

Just a little bit.

WHEN YOU LOOK BACK

When you look back,
may you never see the blaze of a life in ashes because you let
your fear become your fortress, your flaws become your cage
and your imperfect wondrous soul to be imprisoned,
in a tower of self-doubt.

When you look back,
may you never regret the seas you didn't swim in, the beaches
you didn't lose your cares upon, or the moments you hid away
from the world because your body did not meet expectation,
for whom?

When you look back,
may you vividly recall the moments of joy, as the light shone your
way, when the sun came out and the world opened its beauteous
gates to let you wander through its very heart.

When you look back,
may you see that love was enough, love was always the goal, peace
was its chariot and hope the warm wind to speed it along, and may
you share that wisdom with others who so desperately need it.

When you look back,
may you know that your life was one well-lived, that the
heartbreaks you had no control over were the only storms in
your skies and not an unrequited love for your own self, which
darkened your entire journey.

When you look back,
may you breathe easily, safe in the knowledge you blazed a bright
path whilst on this planet, spreading love, spreading light, breaking
and rebuilding and giving of your beautiful self freely.

For that is what you are really here to do.

YOU'VE BEEN GROWING OLDER

You've been getting older since the day you were born.
You wished it faster for many a year,
now you wish it would slow down and stop.

But asking your body to stop getting older,
is begging for your growth to stop too.
Your growth as a human, as a *soul*.

For it's only when you accept how time affects your body,
that you can actually reap the benefits,
of the wisdom it brings alongside.

Each line is a lesson learned or a hardship endured.
Those frown lines were once worries which you fought through.
Or perhaps it's a line of laughter, a wonderful mark to bear.

Each grey hair is a shimmering stripe of life you have *earned*.
A story you can share with those who need to hear,
how you survived.
Your tale could be their saving.

Your purpose as a woman is to age my friend,
to grow more wise, more powerful, more beautiful.

Let the world see the beauty time has in store for you.
Trust that you are who you are meant to be now.
It's time.

You've been *growing* older,
since the day you were born,
what a wonderful thing.

REAL FRIENDS CAN'T BE LOST

You cannot lose real friends.
You just can't.
They won't go, no matter how hard you push them away when
you are not yourself.
They will wait
and wait
and wait,
until they see a tiny glimmer of your light breaking through
and back they will come with open arms.
Your real friends are still there.

And if they feel lost to you right now,
perhaps it's because they are lost to themselves.
Just wait
and wait
and wait,
then knock on that door,
reach in, just in case they can't reach out.
And do it again until they answer.

If you are feeling sad about the people you have 'lost' along the
way my friend,
don't.
They were never yours to keep.
Real friends don't need to be earned, or appeased, or coaxed.
They are in it for the long haul and for all the right reasons.

And each of those friends is worth a dozen fair-weather,
so count your lucky stars if you have even one.

Keep your circle small but let its light be mighty.

You can't lose real friends,
they just won't go.

WOMEN WHO LIKE THEMSELVES

Women who like themselves,
give out a totally different light.

It's like pure unfiltered sunshine mixed with that heady
golden-hour glow you only seem to find on holiday.
As the sun takes its leave of the day and makes way
for the promise of night.

That light,
which makes everything and everyone appear so much more
beautiful, as the air is filled with something special,
something which sparks joy,
deep within your heart.

Seek out the women who like themselves,
for they will like you too.
Their eyes are not the judging kind.

And if you find these women and watch them closely enough,
something magical may just occur,
you may learn how to like yourself too.

Just a little bit.

YOU MUST BELIEVE

I hope you've not forgotten,
how magical life can be?

It's understandable if you have.
Your soul is depleted, weary and worn.

But remember life is capable of so many twists and turns.
And nothing, *nothing*, is permanent.
As fast as you can feel at your very end,
life can throw you a rope and pull you,
to the highest of heights.

It's a rollercoaster.
An up and down, in and out, over and under ride.

This chapter in your story is almost through
and if you can just cast your mind back to the magic,
your silver lining will find you, soon.
And I think it's going to be the most magical time for you.
You've come so far and taken so much.

I hope you've not forgotten how magical life can be my friend.
You must believe.
You must believe.

I WISH YOU WOULD SING

I wish you would sing.
I wish you would dance,
whenever the moment takes you.
I wish that those moments would come more often.

I wish you would ask questions,
unafraid to be seen as ignorant.
I wish you would say sorry without shame,
learn to realise that we are all wrong
and that without mistakes, wisdom cannot grow.

I wish you would stop filtering your words for weakness,
the world needs to hear you, just as you are.
And those moments are pure and joyful.

I wish you would embrace your you-ness,
stop trying to be a copy,
there are enough of those already.

I wish you would loosen your reigns a little my friend,
let the horse bolt from the stable sometimes
and race around the hillside untethered,
because *that's living.*

I wish you would see what I see when I look at you,
wild child of the sun and moon,
full of life and laughter and love.

I wish you would let peace into your heart sometimes,
let all the noise and the bustle fade away
and be as you were always meant to be - happy.

I wish you would see that happiness is a choice
and I wish that once a day at least,
you would choose it.
You just have to choose it.

LET CHAOS RAGE AROUND YOU

Let chaos rage around you,
don't ever let it in.

Like relentless rain on your window,
it should stay outside.

Take comfort in watching it batter and strike,
safe in the knowledge it won't touch you,
unless you let it.

Let chaos rage around you,
don't ever let it in.

Let the world argue back and forth,
whilst you stay dry,
and safe inside.

It's not your burden to be ever right,
leave that to someone else.

If it's your goal to be peaceful,

Let chaos rage around you,
don't ever let it in.

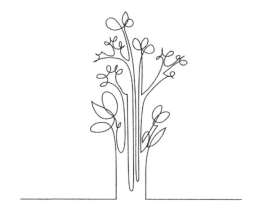

I WANT TO SEE COLOURS

They say comparison is the thief of joy,
and it is.
But it also steals originality.

Comparison kills the unique,
assassinates the exciting,
the new, the outstanding.

Creates rows of soldiers marching in a line.
Identical versions of something
and nothing.

I don't want to see soldiers my friend.
I want to see *you,*
in all your glory,
being fabulously *you.*
In the way that only you can be.

And I want to be *me,*
and I want anyone,
to be *anything,*
they can dare to dream.

I want to see colour and variety,
and all kinds of everything everywhere.

Light up the dull sky with your sparkle
and your fiery bright flames.

The world needs it now,
more than ever.

I AM WATCHING FOR EVERY NEW

They warned me your childhood would whizz by in a flash.
They warned me and I laughed,
because then, each day felt like a lifetime.
Each sleepless night was a year,
each hour of the day was an age.
All my energy was consumed with keeping you alive,
happy and thriving.
Your smiles became my goal,
your laughter my reward,
your tears my every waking concern.

And here we are my love, you have *grown*.
I remember all the *firsts* but I have no idea,
when the *lasts* happened...
Where was I?
The last time you snuggled into my lap to read.
The last time I lifted your warm little body,
to mould into mine so perfectly.
The last time you crawled into my arms,
in the dark of the night.

They warned me your childhood would whizz by in a flash
and I laughed.
But it did, my love,
It did.

And now I watch you grow evermore strong
and I vow to drink in every tiny detail,
lest that go by in an instant also.

I may not remember all the *lasts* my little one,
But I am watching for every *new*.

Yes, I am watching for every new.

I WANT TO HAVE THAT HOME

When my kids are grown and out in the world,
I want to have *that* home,
the one they all travel back to.
The one where everyone feels safe
and joy is bursting out of the windows.
Where a problem shared is a problem halved
and responsibility is left at the door.

The house that rings with laughter, music
and the delighted giggles of children,
or tantrums and tears.
I won't judge, for I remember only too well.

The house that is warm and welcoming and is always messy,
the aftermath of a dinner shared and a drink toasted.

When my children are grown and out in the world,
I will enjoy my solace and my freedom
but I will always, *always*, welcome the noise and the chaos.
And the new friends introduced.
And the new loves.
And the new lives.

When my kids are grown and out in the world,
I want to have *that* home
The one where everyone travels back to, before leaving again,
with their hearts a little more full
and their belts a little too tight.

I want that very much indeed.

HAPPY MOTHER'S DAY

To the women.
Because *all women* have mothered someone at some point in their life, it's just what we do.
We care, we nurture, we mother.

For the mothers who are knee deep in family life, this is your day to feel like a queen, please do. It's entirely deserved and no one needs a day of pampering more. The chores can wait, be rested.

For the mothers who have lost children, this day is another on your *harder* calendar and for that I send you love,
you are so brave.

To the women who no longer have their mother, this day is a heart-breaking reminder of an overwhelming grief. Your mother would want this day to be a time to say her sayings, cook her favourite meal and play her favourite songs. So, please don't avoid that today. I know it hurts but it will help the heal.

To the women who have not made it into motherhood, who so desperately want to. This day is tough, there is nothing you want more than a 3am wake up and a hand drawn card full of love. Please take today to acknowledge all the hard work and energy you have put into your endeavours. I see the hole in your heart and your womb. I see you and I want you to know you're a warrior of love and you deserve so much joy in life. Please let it in.

To the women who mother another child, you are a glorious example of humanity and love.
My heart fills to bursting to witness the gift you give. *Thank you.*

To the women who feel they have not had that maternal love they so crave, forgive. You need your heart whole to make so much love that the future outweighs the past. It starts with you. You deserve it, make it so.

To the women,
ALL the women.
We mother like no other.

IF YOU THINK GRIEF HAS A TIME LIMIT

You have likely never lost,
a piece of your heart.

Everything looks different and will never look the same again.
And that never lessens, we only become accustomed,
to handling it, to *hiding* it.

If you think grief has a time limit,
you have never lost a piece of your heart
and for that, you should be truly grateful.

If you think that the days, months and years will somehow
erase the extent of the loss,
then you have never been unlucky enough to lose a love.
You are blessed, my friend.

For life without that piece of you, is a new life indeed.
It is a new world when the person you miss is no longer here.

Every day is a mountain to climb, battling the waves of emotion,
when a song plays, a smell reminds or a memory rears.

You may think time is healing the hurt, then you enter a new phase
of your life; a relationship, a child, a grandchild, a new opportunity
and you realise you cannot share it with your missing part.

The waves bear down fresh as they were on the very first day.

Let the grieving grieve for as long as they must
and if you want to help,
love them more.

Love is the only way.

TO REACH PERFECTION

If you're trying to reach perfection,
be prepared to try forever.

Perfection isn't a place, or a destination, or a goal.
That's a myth.
That doesn't exist.
You're on a long road to nowhere.

And yet, perfection does occur.
It occurs every day, in fact...

It's in the moments, the minutiae, the ordinary.

It's that feeling when your beloved snuggles in
and two souls become one.
It's the love in a fleeting look that says, '*I got you*'.
It's the table filled with food, family, friends and laughter.
It's the achievement of another battle fought and survived.
It's the smiling eyes that look like your own
and those who went before you.
It's the knowledge that you *can,* no matter what.
It's the safe roof over your head on a stormy night.

There is no such thing as a perfect life my friend,
there are only perfect moments in every day.

The real worry is a life spent chasing perfection,
when actually,
it's passing you by.

In all the little moments,
right here, right now.

I'M A BIG FAN OF WOMEN

I'm a big fan of women with raucous laughs,
women who overshare awkward truths,
when the conversation stalls.

I'm a lover of singing loudly in the car whenever possible
and I love pulling alongside a fellow diva doing the same.

I'm a big fan of women who love women,
who spot lipstick on teeth and help each other out,
when Mother Nature calls.

I'm a huge believer in comparison being the thief of joy,
that dimming someone else's light,
won't ever make yours shine more brightly.

I just can't get enough of those women,
who are unashamedly themselves,
in technicolour glory.

I'm a lover of laughter and those moments,
when the tears of joy start to flow, give me life.

I think the best therapy is quality time with a friend,
who listens without judgement.

I'm a big fan of women who break, who share,
who rebuild each other and cheer along the way.

I'm grateful for this world half-full of fabulous females,
I see you all,
each and every one.

YOU CAN'T GET THROUGH THIS UNSCATHED

You can't get through this unscathed,
that's not how life works.
You're going to get hurt,
you're going to feel loss.

At times you will hit the floor, broken,
crushed by the weight of the pain.
It happens to us all.

But you must keep going,
even if it's the tiniest step each day.

You must keep going my friend,
because if you don't,
how can life bring you that beautiful sunrise,
to usher in the new day?

That day where everything turns around again
and joy rains down on your bruised and battered heart.

The day where you get *your* share of happiness,
your share of love, *your* share of magic.
Your new day.

Everything can flip in a heartbeat, this you know.
As fast as life can throw you in the deep, it can wash you to a new
shore, a shore sweeter than you ever imagined possible.

So hang on in there brave one.

Life is hard, for us all, but it's also beautiful.
And so are you.
So are you.

RESILIENCE

Do we really know what resilience is?
I feel like we're confused.

I've heard people say that hard times create resilient children and I
believe that is true,
IF
Those children are taught to discuss their feelings about the said
hard times.
IF
Those children are coached, understood and helped to evolve
through the hard times.
IF
Those children are given time and patience to transition back into
normality again.

Otherwise it's just trauma that hardens the child so they *appear* to
be more strong.
But really, they are moving on with unresolved damage and the
baggage we are all so familiar with,
from our own unaddressed issues.

So yes,
tough times we have lived through *will* create resilient adults.
I'm sure of it.
Adults who go on to strive and thrive.

But only if we help them get there first.

Resilience isn't looking like you've handled something well,
it's feeling it,
And being *free* of it.

DO YOU SEE THAT WOMAN?

Do you see that woman over there?
The one with confidence and perfect hair.
Last night she paced the floor and couldn't sleep,
she smiles but all she wants to do is weep.

And the lady over there who looks so strong,
is plagued by constant doubts of being wrong.
She wears a mask of bravery and power,
but she curls up like a baby in the shower.

And the one who has a smile as bright as day,
the one who always seems to find a way.
She freely rushes forward to bring comfort,
but cannot find the strength to see her *own* worth.

You see, there's no such thing as *has it all*.
we are all just winging, trying not to fall.
So please don't spend your precious time berating,
you'll miss the wondrous life, *that's waiting*.

PUT YOUR LIFE JACKET ON FIRST

When you feel like you can't go on
and worries are weighing down so heavily,
you fear you may stop breathing.
Take a moment to check,
that those worries are actually *yours* to bear.

You are an empath my friend
and you are currently carrying the weight of the world,
on your two shoulders.

You are not supposed to,
nor can you cope if you continue to do so.
You cannot help others by taking on everything they face,
you will drown.

Face your worries one by one
and identity which is truly your own
and which has come to you via the chaos of the news,
the press and social media.
They must be the first to be put aside.

The world is not yours to fix and you can't,
even if you try.

What you can do,
is keep your little part of the planet calm and safe
and when you are strong again (and you will be),
you can reach out to those who are not.
One by one.

Put your life jacket on first my friend.
It's the only way.

MAYBE YOU COULD START

Maybe you could start each day with a brave heart,
leave the failures of the past on your pillow when you wake.
Maybe you could start each day with a clean slate,
fresh eyes and hope in your soul.

Maybe you could start each day,
by congratulating yourself on getting through,
so many days,
so many weeks,
so many slates wiped,
so many brave new beginnings.

Maybe you could start each day,
with kindness,
for yourself,
first.

Just to see if the thing you have been waiting for,
was always yours to give,
actually.
And not out there,
in someone else's hands,
after all.

YOU ARE A WONDERFUL TWIST OF SCIENCE & NATURE

If you are feeling unworthy today my friend,
consider this.
There were so many ways in which life could have turned
and you may not have come to exist.
Your parents may never have met,
their parents may never have met,
their parents may never have met.

And in each of these sliding door situations,
so many things could have gone wrong,
resulting in another human created and not *you*.
It happens every day.
Separation, war, loss, accident, illness.
Each of your ancestors survived and loved,
to go on and make *you*.

You are a magical, wondrous twist of science, fate and nature.
You are the result of so many love stories
and that mysterious entity of attraction.

This trail of magic and chance can be traced back centuries.
One little change in any of these love stories,
could have wiped out your very existence.
You are a miracle of time,
of so many people who went before you,
You are most definitely born of love.

If you are feeling unworthy today,
look in the mirror and really take in what makes you *you*.
For that was not done easily.

Walk like you have 300 ancestors behind you my friend,
you are finally here.

YOU HAVE COPED

Has anyone told you how well you've done?
How strong you've been?
Because it's true.

Under circumstances you could never have foreseen,
or prepared for,
you have *coped.*

Coping is an underrated word.
It means that you've handled, you've endured,
you've made it through.

Coping is not just *enough,*
it's entirely commendable.

You have coped
and what's more you have helped others to cope.
And even when you felt like you couldn't cope any more,
you did.

You carried on *coping,*
and for that you should be proud.

Whatever else you feel you *should* have achieved in this life,
is not that important.
Not compared to the fact that you're still here.
I care very much about that.

Well done.
You *coped.*

YOU'LL COME BACK

You'll come back to yourself,
after this.
You will.
You'll come back.

It's hard for you to see that right now,
it's been so long.

And chances are, you won't ever be able to imagine
how you *can* come back.
But you will.

This chapter in your life has changed you,
that much is true,
some of those changes were due.

But the parts of you the world needs are still there,
and it's vital that you give them air again.
Let them out, in the sun, again.

Come back however you see fit my friend.
Do it your way,
take your own sweet time.
Just come back.

IF I LET YOU DOWN TODAY

If I let you down today,
I'm sorry.
If I said the wrong thing, or said nothing at all,
when I should have said something meaningful,
I'm sorry.
If I failed to make you smile or turned up late,
or didn't show up at all,
I'm sorry.
If I didn't reply to your message,
or chose the wrong words when I did,
I'm sorry.

I'm spinning plates, my friend.
I'm running on a treadmill that's moving too fast.

I am spinning plates all day every day.
And I am dropping plates.
Lots of plates.

But you must know, my heart is always where it should be.

If I could slow down the treadmill and lay down some plates,
I would be there beside you, answering straight away,
speaking the words you need to hear,
showing up every time and always, *always* making you smile.

And I live in hope, that one day, I will get my plates spinning
far more smoothly and learn how to turn down the speed,
on this machine we call life.

But it's not yet.
Wait for me.
You won't regret it.

TAKE THE PEN

I don't remember when it happened,
the day I realised I couldn't please everyone after all.
The day it sunk in that no-one can truly do that.

If I could remember the day exactly,
I would celebrate it every year.
Like a birthday or a wedding.
Because that was the day I really started to live.
The day I gave myself a gift.

We are not here for a long time my friends,
so if you are living to please, living to pander, living to *fit in,*
you are wasting those precious grains of sand
that swiftly fall through the hole.

Your journey is not the same as those who went before you,
you do not have to follow a path or fulfil an expectation.
Your story should be written *by* you, never *for* you.

Take the pen.
Type the words.
Turn the page.
Open your mind and let your imagination build your future.

For you.

If this chapter isn't bringing you joy,
rewrite it.
It's your book.

DON'T FALL IN LOVE WITH A BODY

Don't fall in love with a body, bodies change.
Fall in love with a twinkle in the eye.
That way, should those blessings ever wane,
you will do your best to bring them back.
And we all need someone who wants to bring back our twinkle,
someone who lives to make us laugh.

Don't fall in love with a body, bodies change.
Fall in love with a mind.
A person's mind only gets more interesting as time moves on.
And should that mind ever lose its memory,
you will do your utmost to be the light that person needs.
You will be their bridge to the past.

Don't fall in love with a body, bodies change.
Fall in love with a heart.
A good heart creates beauty in anyone, anywhere
and spreads more goodness in its wake.
And should that heart ever break,
you will move mountains to put it back together again.

Don't fall in love with a body, bodies change.
Fall in love with a soul.
If you can find a soul you feel connected to,
your life will never be without love.
And should that soul ever leave this earth,
you will still be connected forevermore,
in ways we cannot even begin to fathom.

Don't fall in love with a body,
your body was only ever meant to get you,
where you needed to be.
Fall in love with a friend.

WHATEVER MAKES YOU GLAD TO BE ALIVE

Do that,
whenever you can.

Whatever gives your soul that lift and elevates you,
to a level of harmony, peace and contentment,
chase it and grab it tight.

Stop seeing your life as a chore to be dealt with everyday
and start searching for gaps to put in blissful moments of joy.

Nobody said life had to be this hard.

Nobody made you sign up for a daily grind so punishing,
you couldn't find the energy to do what makes you *happy.*

This life is short my friend and each of us don't know,
how long we have,
so let's not waste another moment of another day,
feeling like a prop in our own show.
We are the stars.
We *are* the show.

Get out there and love your life and if you can't,
make it more loveable.
Change things around.
It's your life.
Do whatever you need to do,
to get any kind of good feeling,
every day.

And start now,
right this minute.
The future is promised to no one,
what are you waiting for?

SOMEWHERE ALONG THE WAY

Somewhere along the way, the world split you in two.
And you keep one half tucked away,
from eyes that may judge.

The other half is presented every day,
like a mannequin, a puppet, a pawn,
going through the motions.

And somewhere along the way,
you decided that this half of you was the one the world wanted.

Perhaps because your other half,
seemed to incite an uncomfortable reaction in others.

Well now you are strong enough little one.
And wise enough to know,
that what you see in those eyes is not disapproval,
it's awe, envy, admiration,
all in disguise.

Let the other side of you out.

She is the one who will take your journey to its final destination,
she is the compass your soul needs,
she is your North Star,
she's your *wild.*

Without her you are simply surviving,
now it's time to live.

Somewhere along the way, the world split you in two.
Let's put you back together again.

TOO MUCH PAIN

You were just in too much pain to keep on living,
and I'm sorry that I didn't see it now.
I think your soul was just too bruised to keep on giving,
you had to take the pain away somehow.

If I'd called you just once more, could I have saved you?
Would my need to have you here, be enough?
Could I have uttered some wise words to help you push through?
Oh how I'll miss my wondrous diamond in the rough.

You were wrong to think the world is best without you,
how could that be when you were just so full of light?
I know your demons made you think life didn't want you,
that you'd be better off surrendering to the night.

You were just in too much pain to keep on breaking,
and I'm sorry that I didn't have the glue.
You smiled so wide no one could ever see you faking,
you had a way of glowing bright that seemed so true.

So may you sleep now love, the best you've ever slumbered,
for you deserve to feel the peace you've never had.
You fought so hard but in the end you were outnumbered,
you feel no pain now and for that at least, I'm glad.

THAT'S SELF LOVE, ACTUALLY

If you silently laugh,
at your own jokes,
in your own head,

that's self-love actually.

If you talk to yourself,
when things go wrong,
the way you would to a child,

that's self-love actually.

If you take yourself away,
when the world is loud,
and let yourself be,

that's self-love actually.

Loving yourself,
as with all forms of love,
is found in the ordinary.

If you silently laugh,
at your own jokes,
in your own head,

that's self-love actually.

You should keep that up my friend,
you should keep all of that up.

MAYBE THEY'RE NOT BEING RUDE

Maybe they're not being selfish?
Maybe they're struggling to cope?

Perhaps, the reason they didn't show up,
was not because you're not important enough,
but because they felt *they* were not important enough.

Perhaps the reason they didn't reply,
is because they were way too deep in the depths
of a suffocating depression,
they cannot bring themselves to talk about.

Perhaps the reason they don't get involved,
is because their anxiety is squeezing the life out of them
and it is all they can do to get through the days.

Perhaps, when they do show up, they do reply
and they do get involved, it's because they managed,
for that one moment, to muster up the superhuman strength
it takes, to win out against their demons.

It's all very well to say 'mental health matters'
but if we are going to shame, shun or reject those
who don't behave the way we want them to,
without questioning whether or not *they are alright,*
then we are a part of the problem.

So, the next time they don't show up.
Reach out.
Be supportive.
It may be the life line they so desperately need.

THE CHANGE

A woman is transformed many times in her life,
the first from little girl,
to something the world would prey upon,
that change brings shock, fear and trouble.
And a woman arises from the ashes of childhood.

The next transformation will bring another human
and that change is so profound,
the world and everything in it, is never the same again.
Your body is no longer yours to covet or keep
and the control you believed you had, may seem to slip away.
Though replaced by something far more precious.

If this transformation is not chosen or gifted,
the change is still just as profound,
as a whole new purpose is found.

Then, ironically, comes *the change,*
Mother Nature's way of telling us,
this time is now for you dear.
Stop overloading, stop over-pleasing, stop giving too much.
Slow down, enjoy more, worry less.
This treadmill you have travelled upon, is too fast and furious,
you're missing the view.

Yes my friend, a woman lives with change from the moment
she opens her eyes and yet, to this day,
we still hear the supposed compliment,
'Oh she hasn't changed.'
And still we see value in those words,
when change is so very much what a woman is about.

And we do it so very majestically,
perhaps we could remark on that instead?

THANK YOU FOR SEEING

Thank you for seeing the good in me,
when I could not.

Thank you for reminding me to laugh,
when I had forgotten how.

Thank you for the times you spent listening,
to my worries, my fears, my insecurities.

Thank you most of all,
for never tiring of all that.

Thank you for being with me,
when I needed you the most,
sometimes in spirit, sometimes literally.

Thank you for never forgetting,
who the real me was,
even though I strayed so far sometimes.

Thank you for enjoying,
the best times of my life with me.

Thank you also,
for showing up during the worst.

Thank you for shining your light,
into my world when darkness had descended.

Thank you,
from the bottom of my heart,
for all of the above.

MORE

You are always so much more than you see.

You are the laughter that rings in the air,
enchanting everyone around you.

You are the softness of your heart,
when troubles are placed in front of you.

You are the words you passed on in times of need,
that stay with each person you gift.

You are the music you hum in the car,
with the windows down and your sunglasses on.

You are a special scent that lingers long after you leave.

You are the memories of childhood stored safely,
like the precious cargo they are,
in the heart of your family.

You are the little girl who fell, who wept, who got up.

You are the friend who stayed when others had gone.

You are so much more than you measured yourself upon.

You are so much more than your failings, your bad days.

Sweet girl, you were always good enough.

The world isn't always good enough for you.

I WONDER

If you've been going about your life,
looking at other women
and thinking,
they're doing so much better than you?

And I also wonder,
if you've been going about your life,
completely oblivious to the fact,
that to someone else,
that woman is you.

Read it again my friend...

To someone else,
that woman is you.

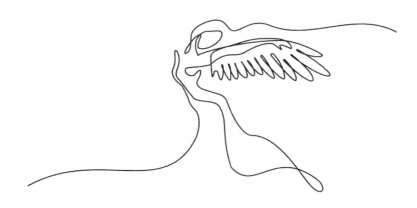

TEXT ME WHEN YOU GET HOME

'Text me when you get home!'
I plead,
as I put her in a taxi.
And then I wait until I hear the ping that means her safety.

'Text me when you get home!'
I yell,
as we walk away in different directions,
just a few yards from our homes,
in streetlight that seems to have no warmth.

'Text me when you get home!'
I beg,
as she leaves me to carry on the party with another,
merry, happy, vulnerable.

'Text me when you get home!'
I say,
then lay down to rest,
fall asleep,
wake up in panic to check for that text.

'Text me when you get home!',
How often do we say those words
and feel like a fuss.
Then someone somewhere doesn't get that text
and we are reminded, heartbreakingly,

that we must always be so.

(Forever remembering Sarah Everard) x

PERFECT IS NOT WHAT I SEE

When I see the perfect people,
perfect is no longer what I see...

I see pressure.
I see stress.
I see strict regimes and unforgiving schedules.
I see fear of failure.
I see hunger.
I see missed fun, empty plates
and lives *too full* with punishing conformity.

Most of all I see a very sad inner child,
who never imagined a life of living up,
to everyone else's expectations.

When I see perfect people now,
I mostly hope that one day,
they will get to enjoy the freedom,
a life without containment can bring.

The joy of removing those shackles and letting go,
of what other people may think of us.

These days, I find my perfect in the real,
the flawed, the fearless and the raw.

For the people who can freely share,
that part of themselves with others,
have found something we all chase,
peace.

IMPOSTER SYNDROME

You're probably sitting there with all the symptoms
of imposter syndrome and you don't even know it.

That feeling of not being good enough,
when you're invited out of your comfort zone.

The anxiety in your stomach when you put yourself out there,
waiting for someone to reveal you as a fraud.

The compliments you ignore because 'they don't really know me,
if they did they wouldn't think that.'

The waiting for someone to realise you're actually a mess
and not as put-together as they think.

Yes my friend, you're probably sitting there,
with all the symptoms of imposter syndrome
and you don't even know it.

Well let me tell you this,
most people give compliments because,
that's exactly what they see and feel.

It's not normal for people to throw accolades around
undeservedly and the reason people think you are really great,
is because *you are.*

So, the next time you hide inside your shell for fear of being
'found out'.
Remember this,
that's your anxiety talking.

It's not real.

IF YOU CAN LOVE

If you can love your children,
when they're behaving in the worst possible way
(that's when they need to feel your love more than ever).

You can love yourself in the toughest times too.

Read that again.

Everyone deserves love,
even when they push it all away,
Even when they act as though your love,
is the last thing they need or want,

that's when they need it the most.

If you can love your children,
when they're behaving in the worst possible way
(that's when they need to feel your love more than ever).

You can love yourself in the toughest times too.

TO THE NEW PARENT

It's going to knock you sideways, the love you feel for that child
and nothing will prepare you for that bolt.
It's everything.

You will be utterly exhausted but humour is going to save you,
look for it when the night is darkest.

You're going to feel inadequate, often, you are no longer in control.
Let it be so, something much bigger is at work now.

Look out for other parents along the way, you need each other.
Judge them the way you'd like to be judged (not at all).
We are all trying our best.

Your child is not an extension of you, you will see something
original there which they brought all by themselves.
Nurture it the most, it is who they truly are.

Life is moving at its fastest now, it will never feel like this again
but strive to find time to listen to the small stuff,
(if you want them to tell you the big stuff when they're older).

Your instinct is key, listen to your own gut.
It's connected to that little human,
and that trumps everything, *trust it.*

Lastly, nobody (and I can't emphasise this one enough),
is doing a better job than you.
However it may seem, they simply are not.

When the dust clears,
you will see that for yourself but for now,
just take my word.

BE AWARE

Right now, you could be driving behind someone,
who is dealing with the worst news of their life.

Be patient.

Today, you could be waiting in line behind someone,
dealing with the end of a relationship,
the loss of a love, the onset of a panic attack.

Be kind.

Be aware, over anything,
this life is a struggle for us all
but for some more than others.

We just don't know what someone is dealing with,
when we lose our patience, our temper.

We just don't know how much a kind word or a smile,
could go to helping that person heal.

Throw out compliments like confetti,
spread smiles whenever you can, they are contagious.

A simple gesture can mean the world to a soul in pain.

A rude comment or a terse remark,
could be the straw that broke the back.

Choose wisely.

Life is short,
we are all in this together.

YOU CAN'T SKIP CHAPTERS

You can't skip chapters in your own story,
that's not how it works.
You have to face each page, each twist, each turn.
You have to live out each and every chapter,
from the start to the end.

Some of those chapters wont be pretty either.
You see, we each get our share of good and bad in this life,
though it may often seem unfairly split.
It really isn't.

We all go through ups, we all go through downs.

Some days we laugh and other days,
we can barely breathe for crying.
There are times when the crying feels,
as though it will never end,
but it will.

And a new chapter will begin when it does,
bringing with it, a very important step in your journey.

And we can't skip them, because if we did,
we wouldn't be who we are now.
And the world needs you just the way you are;
broken, beautiful and a better person for it too.

You can't skip chapters in your own story my friend.
And if you care, or dare, to share your tales
(the good and the ugly),
you may be just the inspiration,
someone else desperately needs today.

So pass it down.

That's how stories work.

TO MY NO-FUSS FRIEND

Thank you for understanding that life is faster than I am.

That, in my mind's eye,
we would hang out so much more often.

Thank you for not passive-aggressively berating me,
each time I fail to return a text or answer a call
and for always allowing me to just dive in
and pick up where we left off,
with a hug, a laugh and some no-fuss friendship.

Thank you for understanding,
that I am barely balancing on this tightrope of adulthood
and when I wobble, thank you for always catching me,
or at least laughing as you pull me from the floor,
that helps too.

It's because of you that our bond will never be broken.

Instead of worrying if I have offended you,
whilst drowning under a pile of life's admin,
I can send my good thoughts out into the ether
and just know,
that *you* know,
I got your back.

And when we do make it into each other's worlds,
it is so very much worth the wait.

Thank you my no-fuss friend,
from the bottom of my heart.

Thank you.

SOFT THINGS

It's okay to be soft,
soft things don't break.
Hard things break,
Snap,
Crack.

Soft things are changed,
squashed a little perhaps
but they yield just enough to last.
And to be a place for someone to rest,
when they need that rest the most.

Yes my friend,
it's really ok to be soft.

Soft is underrated,
and maybe the strongest of all.

Don't let life harden you.

Stay soft.

FOOD FOR THOUGHT

You can avoid alcohol, drugs, sugar, salt, wheat,
dairy and carbohydrates your whole entire life,
You can exercise, meditate
and focus half your day on your health...

But if you are swallowing your dreams,
your ambitions, your regrets, your fears,
your desires and your bitterness on a daily basis,
you will suffer my friend.

For nothing,
nothing,
rots the flesh more,
than the negative emotions,
we ram down our own throats,
on a daily basis.

Food for thought.

Say your truths,
live your own way,
be yourself,
accept who you are,
accept who others are too,
share your dreams,
honour your desires,
chase your ambitions,
or don't.

Perhaps your ambition is quite simply to be peaceful.
Whatever it is you choose to do,
give yourself *peace.*

It's the most healing and rejuvenating path of them all.

JUST A NUMBER

Age means nothing,
it's your energy that counts.
Some people age before their time,
others are endlessly young.
If you fear growing old my friend, stop.
Fear is something which will age you faster.
As is bitterness, regret, envy and greed.
Drop them like hot potatoes,
they are weighing you down and draining your joy.
Embrace your journey and the place you're at.
It's only a number.
Your soul energy will determine how *old* you are.
And if your looks are a worry as the years tick by,
remember, a beautiful young woman,
is a happy accident of nature
but a beautiful older woman,
is carved and chiselled by a life well-lived,
and a heart full of love.

Time can't erase your beauty my friend,
only negativity can do that.

A CRACK IN THE CONCRETE

All you need,
is a crack in the concrete.
To reach up,
reach through,
find sunlight,
find rain.

To escape the darkness,
find air,
again.

You were planted my friend and somewhere along the way,
you went too deep.

You were supposed to thrive, not be buried alive.

All you need is a crack in the concrete.

Keep searching.

Cracks are everywhere,

All you have to do is find one.

Just one.

I'M FINE

I'm balanced on a knife edge, running out of time,
my heart's exploding in my ears but still I say *'I'm fine'*.

I'm hoping you won't notice, yet praying that you care,
my world is turning inside out, no one can reach me there.

I'm swimming for the surface, I'm using all I've left,
the sun is sparkling just above, I'm running out of breath.

I'm balanced on a knife edge, running out of time.
my heart's exploding in my ears but still I say *'I'm fine'*.

I SEE YOU HOLDING SPACE

I see you, holding space for someone.

Maybe someone you once had,
maybe someone you're still waiting for?

I see you, holding space for them and waiting,
waiting for life to begin again.

And I want to tell you to, to beg you even,
to fill that space, my friend.

Fill it with life, with love,
for anyone who is worthy and yourself too.

Fill it with passion, creativity, adventure.
Or even just fill it with peace.

You don't have to hold that space for someone.
They don't need that space.

If they were once alive, they are still within you,
and they won't appear until they see you thriving,
because that is their only wish.

If they are missing from your life,
they will only come back when their time is right.

And if that person is someone you haven't yet met,
they will find their space within you too.
When they get here.

But in the meantime,
fill that space,
it's yours
and you can use it,
for anything you like.

YOU HAVE BEEN SERVED

If you are lucky enough to wake up one day
and feel the pull of something bigger,
something very magical,
inviting you to follow,
go my friend, *go*.

You have been served by Mother Nature.

She comes for us all, when the time is right.

She comes for us all to show us a better,
more peaceful way to be.
A way in which we can actually enjoy this beautiful life
and build ourselves space to flourish,
space to breed joy,
space to exist without expectation.

No more existing she will say, time to thrive.
No more surviving she will add, time to live.

She waits until you are truly done berating yourself,
twisting into a million punishing shapes to please.

She waits until you sit down one day, exhausted again,
and wish for a better way.

If you are lucky enough to feel that powerful hand reach in
and pull you up,
go my friend.

Your moment has arrived
and you won't look back.

YOU SHINE

Because of your struggles, not despite them.

Your own particular beauty,
has been long carved through an intricate series of events,
combined with the wonderful traits that make you *you*,
the people you love and the things which spark your joy.

Your own special light is a source born of the care,
of those who loved you when it mattered most,
what shaped your world along the way,
the fears that keep you awake at night,
the dreams your heart hides
and the little moments that make you glow.

You're a work of art, actually.

And there's only one.
Which makes you pretty much priceless.

You shine because of your struggles my friend,
not despite them.
Let them be a part of you.

YOU'VE BEEN CHANGING

Get comfortable with change my friend,
you've been changing for a very long time
and the world around you has been changing too,
little by little, as well as the people,
all of them.

We just don't notice.

So, when change threatens to whip the rug from under your feet,
or push you out of your comfortable bubble,
face it.

Look change in the eye and let it know that you are *woman,*
you have been changing every day since the day you were born
and you will do so until the day you die.

And you're not afraid.

Remember, the caterpillar doesn't simply go to sleep
and wake up a butterfly.

Inside that cocoon there is a chaotic, ugly mess,
reforming and reshaping
but I bet that little bug feels no fear,
it just follows Mother Nature's lead.

Your cocoon is doing its job.
You have changed.
You've *always been changing.*
You'll change again.

No need to be afraid.

MAYBE

Maybe you can let yourself off the hook today,
if you can?
Somewhere inside of you is a scared little girl,
with a very heavy heart.

She needs your patience too.

She doesn't remember when it became her job,
to have all the answers, to all the questions.

Let her off the hook every now and then,
she does her best.

And actually, she needs you most,
when she she is at her worst.

Maybe you can let yourself off the hook today,
if you can?
Somewhere inside of you is a scared little girl,
who needs a friend.

She needs your kindness too.

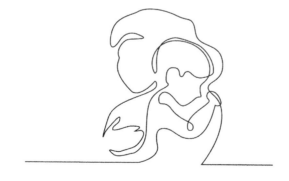

COME HOME

I want to take you back, to the last day you loved yourself.

You were 12, maybe more, maybe less
and until that moment,
thoughts of your body had not existed.
Your life was not marred by the self-doubt you now carry so well.

Something, or someone,
broke a sacred piece of your spirit that day.
Someone with a sharpened tongue, a blackened heart,
or perhaps the blind ignorance of youth.

And each day after, took you further and further away,
from the comfort of your own skin,
the acceptance of your vessel, the synchronicity of your parts.
Until you became so disjointed, you barely recognised the
shapes you saw in the mirror each day.

And as I take you back, I think we can agree,
you were perfect, if perfection exists.
And I think we can agree that if you could,
you would wave a magic wand and give that little girl her joy back,
her confidence back, her clarity of vision.
And watch her fly.

But my friend, it's not too late, never too late, to forgive and heal.
You are simply a wearier version of she.
And you are even more worthy now of the piece they took
from you.
Take it back.

Synchronise your parts, climb back into the comfort of yourself
and fill your skin once more, as though feeling it all for the first
time.

Come home little one,
come home.

SHE LET HERSELF GO

She let herself go, they say.

How wrong they are, how little they know.
She simply stopped fighting time,
stopped fighting nature
and ceased being a slave,
to the unreachable dictations of society,
just briefly.
She focused instead on the real things,
pressing for her attention.
She let herself *in*.
She let herself *rest*.
She let herself *be*.
She let herself *out*.
At no point did she let herself *go*, my friend.
Quite the opposite.
If only they could see it.

If only they could do it too.

COULD YOU?

If you cannot love your body,
could you maybe just accept it?

If you cannot find body confidence,
could you aim for being comfortable in your own skin?

If you cannot achieve self-love,
could you reach self-respect instead?

Because even one of those things will bring about a transformation
so profound, you will wish you started sooner.

The smallest act of kindness, shown to a stranger in need,
can make a gargantuan difference to their day.
This we know.

And sometimes, that tiny act creates ripples,
which travel onward,
and those ripples can become waves,
and those waves can gather momentum,
until they become something *very powerful indeed.*

The same works for you my friend,
the same works for you.

Small acts of kindness,
shown to anyone in need,
makes a huge difference.

So start with you.

If you cannot be your own best friend today,
could you maybe just be nice?

A GIRL NEEDS A MOTHER

Somewhere inside of you, is a little girl who needs a mother.
Whether you have a mother or not,
the need will always be there.
Even if you never had one, if you didn't experience that
maternal love, there is a hole inside of you that perhaps,
you didn't even know you had.

A woman needs a mother, this much is true.

So if you're lucky enough to have a mother living, call her,
listen to her, show up if she wants you, or even if she doesn't.
Let her care, let her in, let her be a part of your life,
for you are an enormous part of hers.

If you no longer have a mother,
be very kind to the little girl who lives within you, she is hurting.
She misses her mother more than you realise.
Be gentle with her and don't be too harsh when she is lost.
She doesn't have a mother to show her the way.

For those of you who have had a mother,
who couldn't love you the way you deserved,
your heart is even more broken and bruised.
There is little in this world more painful than that.
Surround yourself with as much love as you can possibly find.
You deserve it so very much indeed.

You see, a mother is the source of life, the teacher of love,
she is shelter, she is nurture, she is *home*.

Take her with you wherever you go and let her love carry on,
even after she has gone.
It's part of you.
She never really leaves.
If you look within, you will find her there.

Hold on to that, my friend, *hold on to that*.

I hope you liked this book.
I hope you laughed a little and cried a little (both are important).
I also hope that you didn't assume for one moment that I have it all together, because I simply don't.
Nobody does.

Thats why we need each other, right?

You can follow me on social media:
facebook.com/ladiespassiton
instagram.com/ladiespassiton
instagram.com/donnaashworthwordy
twitter.com/donna_ashworth

Email: <u>donna@ladiespassiton.com</u>
Thank you all, *each and every one of you.*

Printed in Great Britain
by Amazon

82010615R00098